CLASSICAL THEMES FOR TWO

Arrangements by Peter Deneff

ISBN 978-1-5400-1417-7

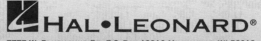

7777 W. BLUEMOUND RD. P.O. BOX 13819 MILWAUKEE, WI 53213

In Australia Contact:
Hal Leonard Australia Pty. Ltd.
4 Lentara Court
Cheltenham, Victoria, 3192 Australia
Email: ausadmin@halleonard.com.au

Visit Hal Leonard Online at
www.halleonard.com

ACADEMIC FESTIVAL OVERTURE

CELLOS

By JOHANNES BRAHMS

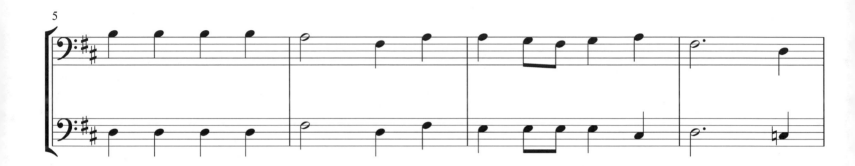

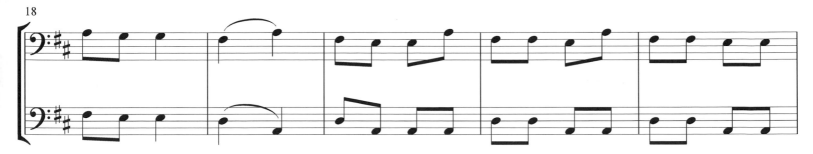

AIR
from WATER MUSIC

CELLOS

By GEORGE FRIDERIC HANDEL

Andante con moto

(small notes optional)

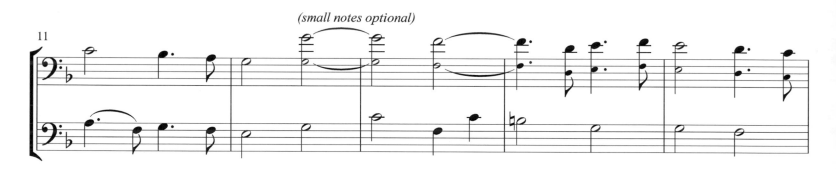

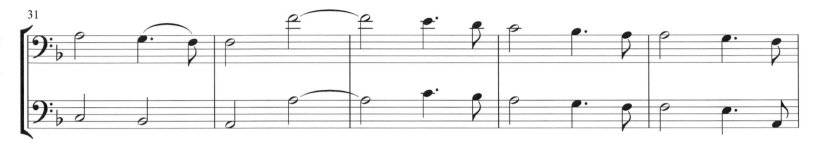

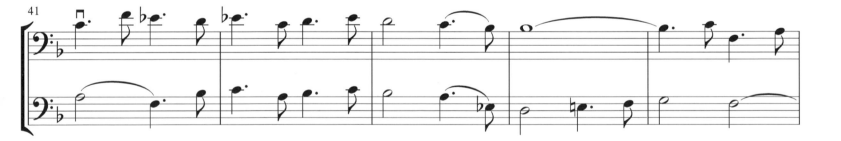

AIR ON THE G STRING

from ORCHESTRAL SUITE NO. 3 IN D MAJOR, BWV 1068

CELLOS

By JOHANN SEBASTIAN BACH

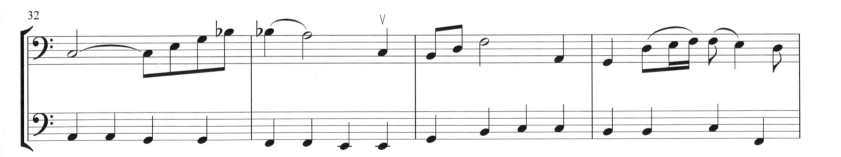

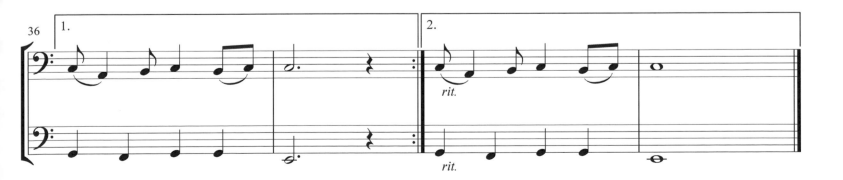

BLUE DANUBE WALTZ

CELLOS

By JOHANN STRAUSS, JR.

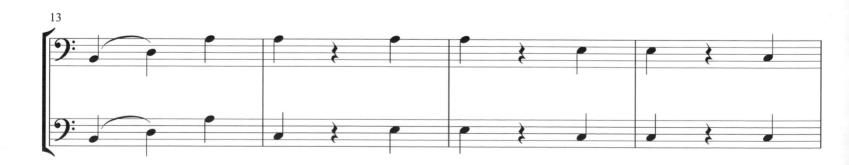

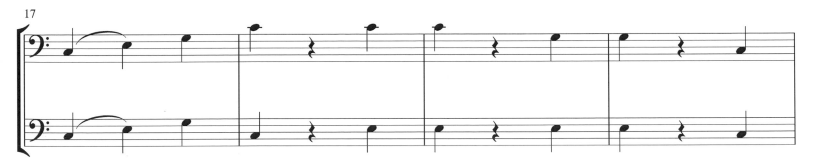

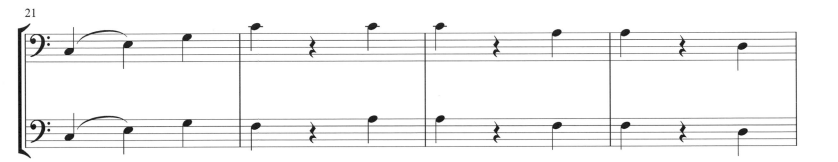

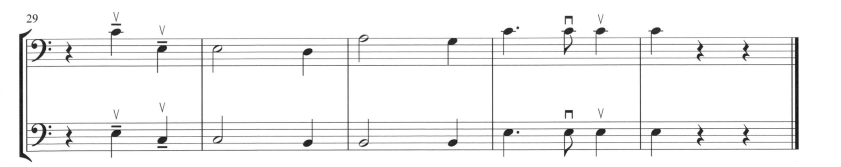

CANON IN D

CELLOS

By JOHANN PACHELBEL

CLAIR DE LUNE
from SUITE BERGAMASQUE

CELLOS

By CLAUDE DEBUSSY

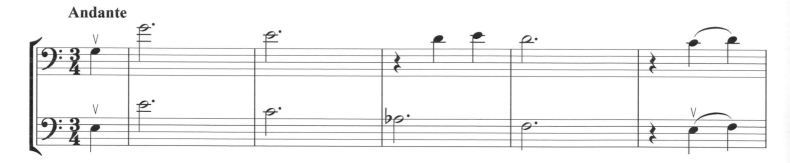

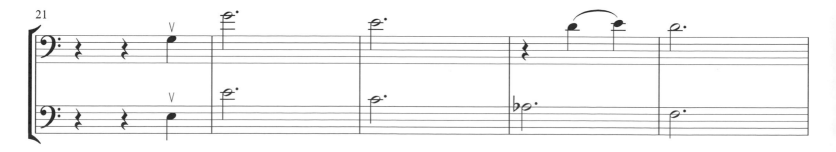

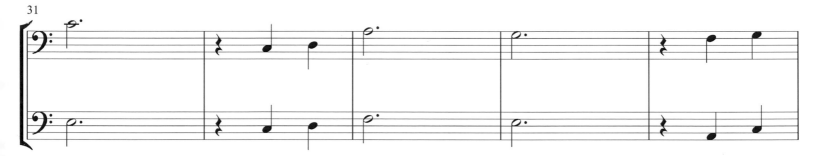

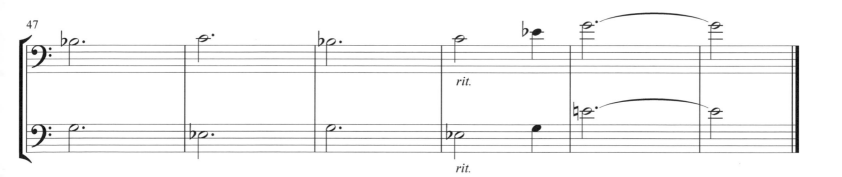

EINE KLEINE NACHTMUSIK
(Second Movement Theme: "Romance")

CELLOS

By WOLFGANG AMADEUS MOZART

FLOWER DUET
from LAKMÉ

CELLOS

By LÉO DELIBES

Andante con moto

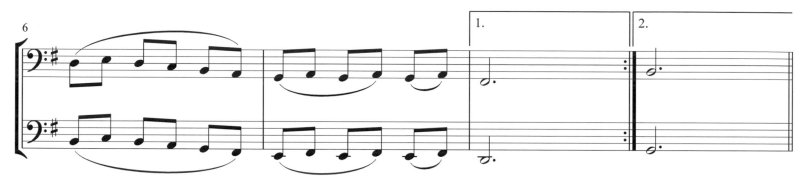

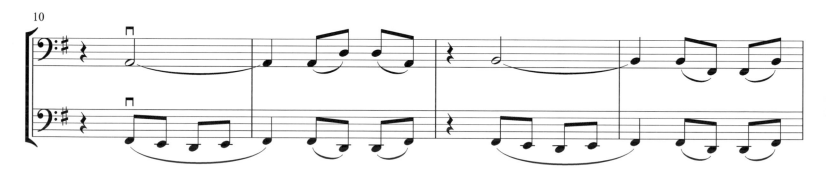

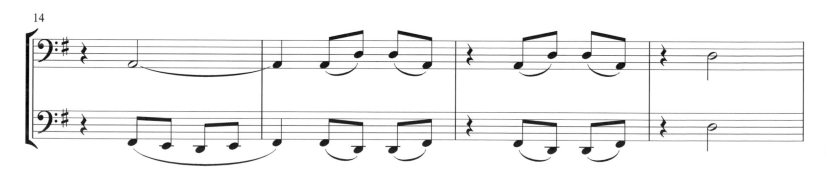

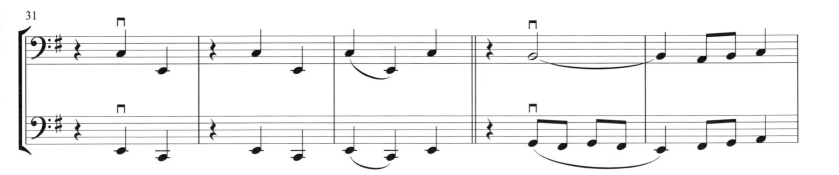

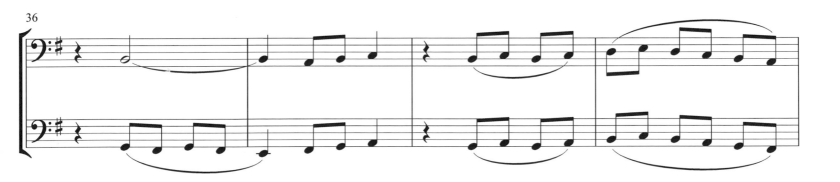

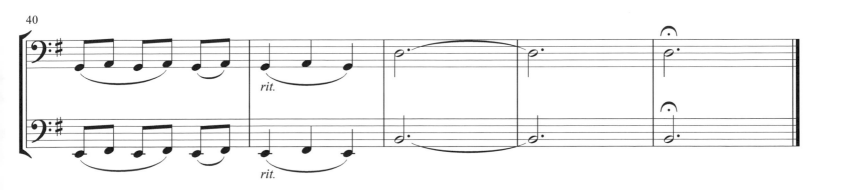

HALLELUJAH CHORUS

from MESSIAH

CELLOS

By GEORGE FRIDERIC HANDEL

Allegro

(small note optional)

rit.

rit.

HORNPIPE
from WATER MUSIC

CELLOS

By GEORGE FRIDERIC HANDEL

Allegro maestoso

HUNGARIAN DANCE NO. 5

CELLOS

By JOHANNES BRAHMS

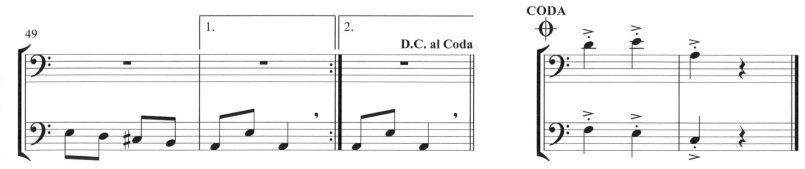

JESU, JOY OF MAN'S DESIRING

from CANTATA 147

CELLOS

By JOHANN SEBASTIAN BACH

D.C. al Coda

CODA

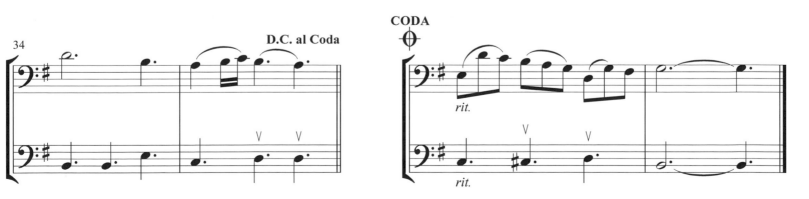

rit.

MARCH
from THE NUTCRACKER

CELLOS

By PYOTR IL'YICH TCHAIKOVSKY

March tempo

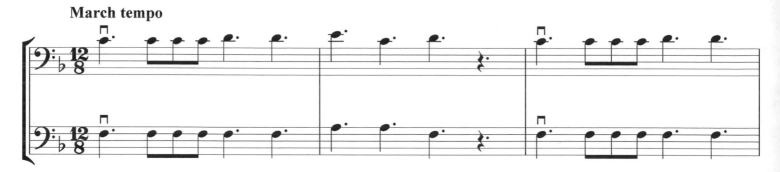

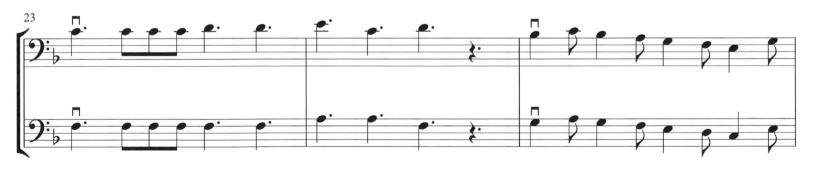

MINUET IN G
from ANNA MAGDALENA NOTEBOOK

CELLOS

By CHRISTIAN PETZOLD
formerly attributed to J.S. Bach

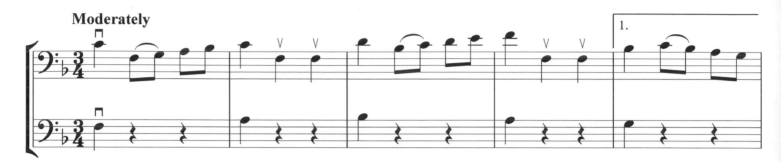

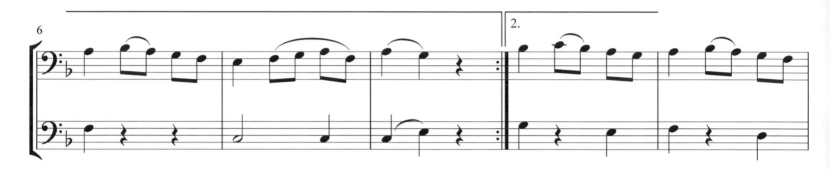

ODE TO JOY

from SYMPHONY NO. 9 IN D MINOR

CELLOS

By LUDWIG VAN BEETHOVEN

MORNING
from PEER GYNT

CELLOS

By EDVARD GRIEG

Allegretto pastorale

PICTURES AT AN EXHIBITION
(Promenade)

CELLOS

By MODEST MUSSORGSKY

POMP AND CIRCUMSTANCE
March No. 1

CELLOS

By EDWARD ELGAR

Allegro

RONDEAU
from SUITE DE SYMPHONIE

CELLOS

By JEAN-JOSEPH MOURET

Moderately

SHEEP MAY SAFELY GRAZE

from CANTATA 208

CELLOS

By JOHANN SEBASTIAN BACH

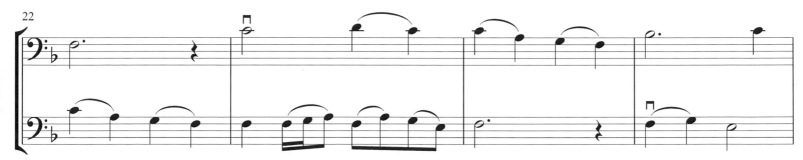

THE SURPRISE SYMPHONY
(Symphony No. 94, Second Movement Theme)

CELLOS

By FRANZ JOSEPH HAYDN

SYMPHONY NO. 7
(Second Movement Theme)

CELLOS

By LUDWIG VAN BEETHOVEN

Allegretto

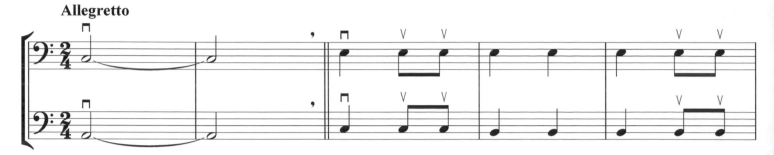

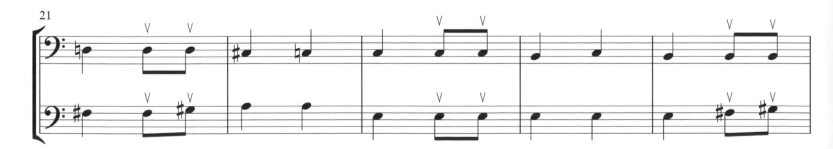

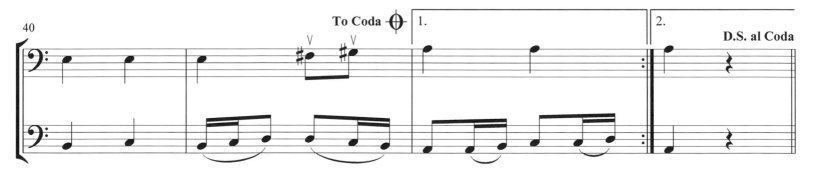

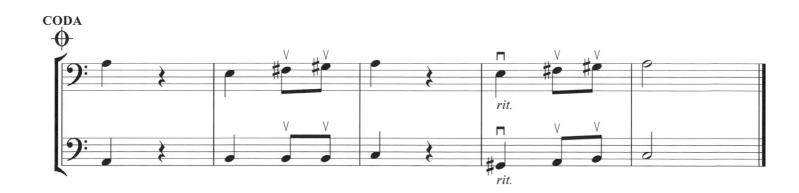

TRUMPET VOLUNTARY
(Prince of Denmark's March)

CELLOS

By JEREMIAH CLARKE

Moderately

WILLIAM TELL OVERTURE
(Theme)

CELLOS

By GIOACHINO ROSSINI

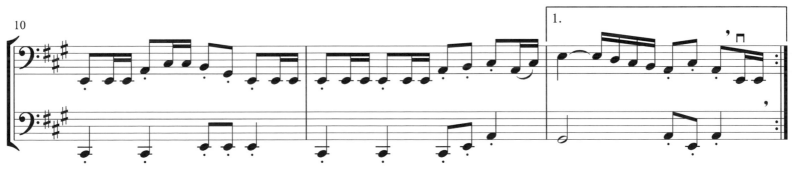

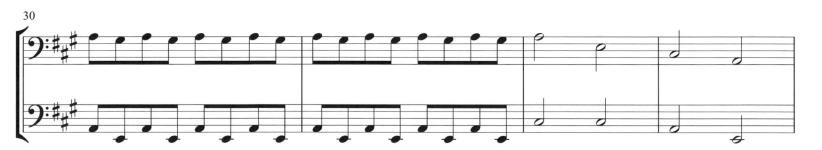